To: Bady

From: Marsmah

Date: 1000000000

PO Box 1599, Vereeniging, 1930, RSA

1025 N Lombard Road, Lombard, IL, 60148, USA

First edition 2011

Cover designed by Christian Art Kids

Images used under license from Shutterstock.com

Set in 16 on 20 pt Chalkboard by Christian Art Kids

Printed in China

ISBN 978-1-77036-730-2

11 12 13 14 15 16 17 18 19 20 – 10 9 8 7 6 5 4 3 2 1

Blessings for Little Ones

Carolyn Larsen

christian art kids

Blessings, blessings everywhere!

God made a beautiful
world for me.
I love all the different
kinds of flowers.
They are so colorful
and they smell so good.
I like the cute little birds
that sing happy songs too.
Everything God made
is a blessing to me!

Chores are a blessing

I walk my dog every day.
I am glad that this is my very own chore.
I am learning to be responsible
by taking care of my pet.
I am learning to do things
even when I don't feel like it.
I am learning to be all grown-up.
That's a blessing!

Joyous blessings

Blessings, blessings everywhere!
And every one is a gift from God!
He gave me my family and friends.
He surrounds me with
laughter and love.
He shows me happiness and joy.
God shows His love
every day by everything
He gives to me!

Blessings of miracle growth

It is amazing!
I put a little seed in the ground;
cover it with soil;
water it and wait.
God makes that little seed
grow and grow,
until pretty soon I have
my very own vegetables.
The miracle of gardening
is such a blessing!

Presents are blessings

I love to get presents!
A present means someone
is thinking about me.
A present means
someone loves me!
I love to give presents too!
Presents are fun.
They make me happy!
Presents are blessings!

Good night blessings

I am never afraid when
I go to sleep at night.
No scary shadows.
No bad dreams.
God promises to take
care of me and I know
He is always with me.
A peaceful night of sleep
is a blessing from God!

Learning is a blessing

My mommy and daddy
read books to me.
I love cuddling while we read.
We read book after
book after book.
I almost have some
of them memorized.
I learn things from
every book we read.
Learning new things is a blessing!

Family is a blessing

My brother plays
soccer with me.
My sister sings silly songs
that make me laugh.
It is fun to have
a brother and a sister.
Even on the days when
we don't get along,
we love being a family.
Brothers and sisters
are a blessing!

Fun-filled blessings

Skateboarding. Climbing.
Running. Jumping.
These are some of my
favorite things to do!
Sometimes I fall down
and get scrapes and bruises.
But I always get up
and try, try again.
It is a fun blessing to be
able to do my favorite things.

Even being sick is a blessing

Ugh! I am sick with a cold.
My head hurts and
my throat is sore.
I feel terrible and
all I want to do is sleep.
But being sick reminds
me to be thankful
for when I am well.
Feeling healthy and strong
is really a blessing!

Blessings of love

I cannot be quiet. I have to sing.
I want the world to know
that I love God!
Every day He shows
how much He loves me.
His blessings are everywhere.
Each one makes me
feel special and loved.
It is a blessing for me
to be able to say,
"I LOVE YOU, GOD!"

The blessing of sharing

I do not have a kitten
but my friend does.
Her little kitty is very sweet.
My friend knows that
I would like to have a kitten.
So she lets me
play with her kitty!
My friend is sharing
and that is a blessing to me!

Being a blessing to others

God blesses me every day.
He gave me family
and good friends.
I want to share
His blessings with others.
I can do that by being kind,
sharing my things,
and giving presents.
I can be a blessing to others!

The blessing of God's love

The biggest blessing ever
is to know that God loves me.
He really does.
No matter what I do –
if I am grumpy or happy.
He loves me whether
I obey or disobey.
He loves me when
I am asleep or awake.
He loves me all the time!

Sharing love is a blessing!

I can share God's love with others.
He gave me friends to play with.
I can show love to them!
He gave me a wonderful family.
I can show love to them!
Sharing God's love with
others is a fun, fun blessing!

Friendly blessings

A new girl came to my school.
She did not have any friends
and I felt sorry for her.
I was kind of scared
but I talked to her anyway.
She is nice!
Now I have a new friend.
It is a blessing to be friendly to others.

School is a blessing!

School is so much fun!
My teacher is really great.
I have lots of friends at school.
I learn new things every day.
I find new things that I am
good at every day too!
I am glad I can go to school.
School is a blessing.

Failure is a blessing

I like to learn new things.
Sometimes I get frustrated
when I do not learn things fast.
It makes me sad to fail.
But it also makes me work
harder and harder
until I learn a new thing.
So failure is a blessing because
it makes me work harder!

I am a blessing

It is good to take care of myself.
That means brushing my teeth,
taking a bath, getting enough sleep,
and eating good food.
Mommy says my body is
the temple of God. That is a good
reason to take care of it.
Taking care of myself is a blessing.

Christmas blessings!

I love Christmas!
I love the decorations
and the cookies and the music
and the parties and the presents.
It is my favorite time of year.
Most of all I love Christmas
because that is when
we celebrate Jesus being born!
That is the best blessing of Christmas!

The blessing of a new day

Yippee! It is the morning
of a brand-new day!
I wonder what will happen today?
I hope I have time to
play with my friends!
It is going to be so much fun!
I am thankful that I have
a brand-new day to enjoy
after a good night of rest!

Friends are a blessing

Friends make life so much fun.
It is a blessing to have
a friend I can talk with.
We share secrets.
We laugh together.
I can tell my friend anything.
God must have known how
important friends would be.
Talking with my friend is one of
the best blessings He gave me!